Self Help In Sight

Self Help In Sight

Self Help with Relationships and Relationship Loss

R. Brad Lebo, Ph. D.

Printed in the United States of America

ISBN 978-0-578-00090-9

Contents

Introduction

Long before entering graduate school I was interested in not just being "okay." Whether it was about how to eat, how to exercise, or how to relate to others, I searched for expert advice on how to be or do better.

Perhaps you can imagine my surprise when I learned that my graduate school curriculum would not include any information on psychological wellness. The focus was exclusively on illness and symptoms of illness. There was comparatively little information about what it meant to be or feel other than ill. I was forced to supplement my curriculum to learn what leading experts thought about "above average" or "optimal" functioning.

My suspicions are that not much has changed in both mental health graduate schools and physical health (medical) graduate schools. Perhaps it takes a lot of time to study illness in its various forms, not leaving enough time for the study of wellness and being healthy. Whatever the reason, promoting mental, emotional, and physical wellness takes a back seat to treating illness.

Try a test to see the status of wellness or optimal health yourself. Go to your local physician or mental health provider and tell him or her that you are well, but you want to be better--better able to relate to others, fitter, more resilient to disease, or whatever else you are interested in being better at. Let me know what they tell you, if they are able to tell you anything.

So, in the spirit of promoting wellness, this short book offers help on recovering from the loss of a relationship as well as on forming healthier or more optimal relationships. It is written with two goals in mind: (1) recovering from a loss as quickly as possible and (2) getting better at entering and sustaining relationships, thereby reducing the chance of feeling the emotional pain or despair of relationship loss again.

While I cannot guarantee you will never be hurt by relationship loss again, I can guarantee that if you do the work recommended here, your chance of being hurt will decrease markedly.

Some of the advice given here applies in the case of a loved one passing. Some of it applies to relationships that are not romantic love relationships (for example, your relationship with your boss, a parent-child relationship, or a friendship). The fact that the advice applies does not mean that it is the best advice for situations other than romantic love relationships. While the same broad strokes apply to most relationships, the details differ depending on the nature of the relationship.

If you have questions about a loved one passing, a

boss/subordinate relationship, or a parent/child relationship, let me know, and I will generate specific advice for these situations. If there is enough interest or demand, I will write a similar book with other types of relationships in mind.

Now, without further delay, I'd like to introduce the four essential parts to this short book: (1) Part one covers steps to take today to help your self deal with the "loss of relationship" with someone you love or cared about. It is an attempt to acknowledge the emotional pain you are likely feeling while starting the recovery process through self-care, self-reassurance, and the start of acceptance.

(2) Part two covers increasing your acceptance of your loss and figuring out "who you are" so that you have a good feeling about your self and start to see good in others and the world.

(3) Part three covers starting the process of imagining or visualizing a future romantic partner and consolidating your sense of who you are (making it clearer). Although I am not inclined to be mystical, I do believe that you cannot see what you don't first visualize being possible.

(4) Part four covers starting a new love relationship and touches on the points of being true to your self, when to start a new relationship, and what

successful relationships look like.

Your current emotional state is the best indicator of where in this book you should be spending your time. If you have recently experienced a breakup, go to Part One until you are feeling up to rejoining the social world. If you've recovered from a breakup and are moving toward a new relationship, spend your time in Parts Two, Three, and Four. These sections are there to help you build a solid foundation for relating well with others and to avoid feeling the emotional pain or despair that follows relationship loss in the future.

Please enjoy the pages that follow and contact me with questions. I wish you well.

Dr. Brad Lebo
drlebo@selfhelpinsight.com

SELF HELP IN SIGHT

Part One
First Things First

First Things First

☼

"Faith is taking the first step, even when you don't see
the whole staircase."
Martin Luther King Jr. (1929 – 1968)

The Role of Faith:

Having faith in the recommendations that follow
makes all the difference because there is often a delay
between taking a step in the right direction and feeling
the benefit of the step. Sometimes a recommendation
will make immediate sense to you; other times not. In
each case, have faith that the recommendation being
made is based on research and/or experience. The
recommendations will work. Give them your best
effort, and have faith.

A Few Words about Self-Help:

Self-help is defined[1] as: care for or betterment
of one's self by one's own efforts, as through study.

---

1   http://www.yourdictionary.com

Self-help is a unique way to help yourself feel better or get better at something. It is different than going to a physician, a physical therapist, a coach, or a psychotherapist, professionals who work or partner with you to help you feel or get better.

In contrast, self-help depends exclusively on your personal ability to study information and put what you learn into practice. Self-help is not a replacement for going to an expert, but it can supplement the help of an expert and is, in general, a better strategy when you are striving for exceptional performance.

For example, seeking the help of a golf professional when learning to play golf is an excellent way to start. Once you learn the basics from the professional, you will benefit from practicing the skills of golf and studying how the best in the world play. Through practice and study, you are helping yourself get better than you ever would by just taking instruction from the professional. Your self-help causes you to learn the skills more completely than if you depend on someone else. In addition, you get exposed to a broader variety of approaches to a particular skill than if you have only one instructor.

Perhaps a more relevant example for this book is learning how to manage anxiety. You are likely to benefit from an expert's input on the basics of managing anxiety. You are also likely to get better at managing anxiety if, after mastering the basics, you study additional strategies for managing anxiety and work at implementing them.

So, the cognitive strategies that you might learn from a psychologist are supplemented by regular exercise, progressive relaxation techniques, or mindful disciplines like yoga, all supplementary strategies for managing anxiety.

The point is that self-help can be a powerful ally in anyone's effort to feel better or get better at something. The formula is to master the basics with help, then move into the more complex and refined strategies for doing better than average. Expert help points you in the right direction. You then can actively work to get better and become your own expert.

Without Further Ado--First Things First:

If your heart is breaking because of a lost love, if you've been betrayed, abandoned, "dumped," or you know you must leave a relationship because of abuse, you certainly are not alone. Relationships coming to an end is common. Even if we look only at divorce rates, "50% percent of first marriages, 67% of second, and 74% of third marriages end in divorce."[2] Countless other romantic relationships end every moment of every day and, in most cases, someone feels emotional pain, despair, loss, and heart break.

So, what to do? The answer is:

One--Take Care of Your Physical and Emotional Self:

You take care of your self by doing each of the following:

- Move your body. In case it is not obvious why this is a recommendation, let me note that no less and authority than the US Surgeon General reported an association between physical exercise and a sense of psychological well-being.[3] Regular exercise increases physical and emotional tolerance of stressful events. Moving your body will help fight off feelings associated with anxiety and depression. Take a walk, jog,

---

2 This is according to Jennifer Baker of the Forest Institute of Professional Psychology in Springfield, Missouri as quoted in 2008 on www.divorcerate.org.

3 U.S. Department of Health and Human Services. (1996). *Physical Activity and Health: A Report of the Surgeon General*. Atlanta, GA: U.S. Department of Health and Human Services, Centers for Disease Control and Prevention, National Center for Chronic Disease Prevention and Health Promotion.

run, swim, or bike. Get moving to start the
process of feeling better. Continue moving
every day to keep your progress going.

- Please note: Check with your physician if you
have any doubt about your ability to start an
exercise program safely. The goal of the advice
to "move your body" is to make you healthier,
not to cause you a medical problem.

- Eat well. After a relationship ends, you might
feel like overeating, like not eating at all, or
like binging on "high sugar" foods (for example,
ice cream and chocolate). The goal of the
advice "eat well" is to eat healthy foods in
moderate quantities despite not wanting to eat or
wanting to do nothing but eat. Healthy eating is
consistent in my mind with the advice of
Micheal Pollan: "Eat food. Not too much.
Mostly plants."[4] This is not the place to get an
education on how important diet is in your
overall health. I am confident your definition of
healthy eating is closer to Pollan's than not,
even if you don't always eat in a way that you
know is best. Now is an especially important
time to help your self by eating well, not as you
might want to or even maybe as you are used to,

4 Pollan, M. (2008). *In Defense of Food: An Eater's
Manifesto.* New York: Penguin Press.

but as you know you should.

- Avoid self-medicating with alcohol or drugs. This is stating the obvious. I hope you are not learning here that alcohol and drugs do not solve any problems and often compound any problems you do have. As tempting as numbing your self to pain through alcohol and drugs may be, avoid giving into temptation. Doing otherwise will, 99 times out of 100, just slow down your recovery.

- Get rest. Getting adequate sleep is critical to maintain your resilience in the face of stress. In the book, *Making a Good Brain Great*, author Daniel G. Amen notes that "getting less than six and a half hours of sleep at night decreases our ability to fight stress."[5]

  A relationship loss is one of the most stressful events a person can face. Take care of your self. Sleep eight hours or more if at all possible. Avoid caffeine and sugar-rich foods before bedtime if you have trouble falling asleep. Do what you can to relax before bedtime. For example, practice yoga or meditation. If you toss and turn once in bed, find ways to distract your self with "white

---

5 p. 170. Amen, D. G. (2005). *Making a Good Brain Great*. New York: Three Rivers Press.

noise," music, or non-stimulating reading. Think ahead about what will help you get to sleep and take whatever steps you need to in advance. Restorative sleep is as much a "cure-all" as regular exercise. Pay attention to doing all you can to take advantage of its power to aid recovery.

- Seek the support of a network of friends. In the book, *Why Zebras Don't Get Ulcers: A Guide to Stress, Stress-Related Diseases, and Coping*, author Robert M. Sapolsky carefully distinguishes between relationships with supportive friends and relationships with everyone else. Regular contact with supportive friends and family members can reduce the harm caused by stress. Contact with friends or others who are not supportive does not reduce the harm caused by stress and may make things worse.[6] His advice is "to find sources of social affiliation and support [and to] be patient; most of us spend a lifetime learning how to be truly good friends and spouses."[7] This is good

---

6 Sapolsky, R.M. (1993). *Why Zebras Don't Get Ulcers: A Guide to Stress, Stress-Related Diseases, and Coping.* New York: W. H. Freeman and Company.

7 p. 280. Sapolsky, R.M. (1993). *Why Zebras Don't Get Ulcers: A Guide to Stress, Stress-Related Diseases, and Coping.* New York: W. H. Freeman and Company.

advice. Choose your support network wisely and get connected!

- Take vitamins and prescribed medications. Vitamins, if part of your normal routine, can help maintain your physical well being and may improve your resilience during a stressful period. If nothing else, taking vitamins that you are in the practice of taking is one of many ways to demonstrate self-care to your self. You can say, "I am doing this to take care of my self. I am worth being taken care of, and this is something that I can do for my self." The same logic applies to prescribed medications.

- Maintain your routines, including your work, hobbies, exercise routines, and social routines. Often after a relationship loss, it is difficult to maintain personal routines. Indeed, loss of interest in normal activities is common and a symptom of clinical depression should it persist. Fight the urge to do nothing. Go through the motions at first to get back to a routine. Doing so will get you out of the house, keep you busy, help you avoid obsessive thoughts about your loss, and may help you feel you will survive, that there is a light at the end of the tunnel of emotional pain.

Follow each of the recommendations listed above to improve your care of your physical and emotional self. Following the specific recommendations should speed your recovery.

Think of each recommendation as an affirmation of your worth. You deserve the best care you can give your self. When you take care of your self, you are saying to the world, "I am worthy of being cared for and am doing what I can for my self." If you value your self in this way, it makes it easy for other people to value you as highly.

Two--Take Additional Care of Your Emotional Self by Repeating Over and Over Again, "I will get through this and feel better":

If you have never been through a breakup before, tell your self that others, perhaps even close friends of yours, survive breakups and soon start feeling much better.

If you have been through a breakup before, remember the experience from the first moments of loss through your transition to feeling better and presumably to being "in love" again.

You should find comfort in knowing that you

will get through any emotional pain or despair to feeling better. In many ways, getting through a breakup is a kind of surviving. You can do it, you will get through it to better times.

Remind your self of the transition from feelings of despair to feelings of acceptance frequently, even if you have never before made the journey. If it helps, write "I will feel better" over and over in a journal. Write it on index cards and tape the cards in places you will see often, record the statement "I will feel better (survive)" and use it for your ringtone. Tell others that you will survive until both you and they believe it, or have a close friend repeat the statement to you until you can no longer stand to hear it.

Do not underestimate the power of these affirmative statements. If you do nothing else, you should remind your self when feeling low that you will feel better again. The vast majority do.

If, despite consistent effort, you do not come out of the feeling of despair, seek professional help. Normally, people recover from loss without entering a state of clinical depression. Of course, sometimes people do not recover and become clinically depressed. If that is the case for you, seek professional help.

Depression is a treatable condition. If

untreated, clinical depression can lead to death. Normally, professionals expect individuals to feel a lessening of their emotional pain or despair within two weeks.

It bears repeating, if you feel no relief despite your consistent efforts to take care of your self, seek professional help. It may take longer than two weeks to feel something close to full relief. The point is, normal grieving means feeling less depressed as time passes. If you have a doubt about how quickly you are "bouncing back," again, seek professional help.

Three--Start Working on Acceptance of Your Loss:

Acceptance is the third priority in a recovering from relationship loss program for a reason: it is less important than taking care of your physical and emotional self. At the same time, acceptance is the path to full recovery. From the first days, "float" the thought, "I can accept this outcome and move on."

The concept of acceptance is as old as self awareness. It has prominence in many spiritual teachings and is central to both Taoism and Buddhism. It means experiencing a situation or set of circumstances without seeking a change. When a relationship has ended it means experiencing the loss without fighting or yearning for a different outcome.

Acceptance does not mean not feeling sad. Acceptance can take the sting out of "bad" feelings, however. The idea is to start moving toward accepting what can't be changed.

Your success at accepting what can't be changed, can help the process of recovery by decreasing the intensity of your distress. You may go as far as achieving total acceptance as promoted in Taoism or Buddhism, but you don't have to go that far to start feeling better.

So, in addition, to constantly repeating to your self, "I will get through this," occasionally muse about accepting circumstances that you cannot change. Doing so will aid your recovery and get you to the point where you can restart thinking about being in a romantic relationship.

Part Two
Restarting

Restarting

☼

"Acceptance is such an important commodity, some
have called it 'the first law of personal growth.'"
Peter McWilliams (1949-2000)

More about Acceptance:

As you move toward feeling your old self and
you are beginning, even if grudgingly, to accept your
loss, it is time to work on acceptance and the
mindfulness that aids it. Doing so restarts the process
of thinking about being in a relationship. It is like
clearing the clutter out of a house before remodeling
it.

Truly accepting the end to a relationship
requires (1) that you believe that it is beneficial not to
fight the "tide" or to try to change things that are
hard, if not impossible, to change, and (2) that you
remain aware or mindful of your thoughts and
feelings, noticing when they return to thinking of or
wanting things to be different.

My assertion is it is beneficial to avoid trying to

change things that are hard to change. This assertion is based on the observation that trying to change others, and particularly others who want to end a relationship, frequently ends up being painful and futile. You are likely to reap only anger and sadness for your trouble. This outcome seems likely even if you invest huge amounts of time and emotional energy.

You may have heard the phrase, "you can't change someone else." The fact is that you *can* change someone else. We do it all the time. Indeed, all of us frequently influence others to think and behave differently. If I could not influence you, there would not be any point in writing this short book.

The statement to make is, "you can only change someone else if he or she is (1) motivated and (2) able to change."

During a breakup, the person initiating the breakup is rarely, if ever, both motivated and able to change. If he or she were, the breakup would not happen.

This all means that trying to reverse a relationship breakup is likely a waste of time and energy and will probably only leave you angry and sad. In other words, it is beneficial to accept the loss of a relationship.

Instead of trying to change the outcome of a

breakup, spend your time and energy trying to change your self and your outlook by (1) learning who you are and (2) visualizing your new partner.

The time you spend working on your self is going to help you more than any time you spend trying to change how someone else feels about you.

Awareness, mindfulness, or just plain old "paying attention to your thinking," is a great ally because of the mind's tendency to return to thinking or feeling about a lost love. Indeed, the mind can be a powerful adversary when it comes to trying to move on emotionally.

Obsessive thoughts are an example of how powerful an adversary the mind can be. Obsessive thought patterns are pretty common in the days and sometimes months after a breakup.

The antidote for both obsessive and less intense thinking and feeling about a relationship loss is awareness or mindfulness. If you are mindful, you can redirect your thinking about your loss or your ex before it builds momentum. In the first days after a breakup this may be hard to do, but if you stick with it, it will get easier.

The goal is to catch your self early and purposely redirect your thoughts. You can redirect your thoughts back to whatever you are doing (the "now" or the "present") or to plans for taking better care of your self, or to plans for learning more about your self.

The point is to consciously and purposefully redirect your thoughts. Doing so will have the effect of speeding your recovery because you will spend less time in anger or sadness.

In summary, acceptance of one's circumstances and loss is a critical step in recovery because of the relief from anger and sadness it provides. The rate of your recovery will be increased if you stay aware of when your mind returns to thinking about or feeling the pain of your loss. The sooner that you can redirect your thinking to something other than your loss, the sooner you will recover.

Allowing your self to feel sadness over a lost love is fine, even healthy. Wallowing, or becoming immobilized by feelings of despair or obsessive thoughts, is not healthy and should be avoided with the help of acceptance and awareness.

Finding Out Who You Are:

Most people know who they are, right? Not so much. It seems easy to know one's self, but it is not easy. It is difficult to know who you are. The chief reason it is difficult, is because of the confusion created by parental and societal messages of who you should be.

We are bombarded from the moment we are born with messages of who we should be and how we should behave. The amount of information of this sort we are exposed to today is literally overwhelming.

If you have trouble seeing this point, think of the last time you wanted to or did something that was "outside the norm" or what is "expected of you." Perhaps you wanted to wear your comfortable shoes to work or did not feel like going to visit your parents on Thanksgiving, or wanted to see your "friends" instead of your "boy/girlfriend." The point is that there are stated/obvious and unstated/subtle messages coming from society, family, employers, and partners all the time. For example, advertising has a part in defining what is attractive and therefore shapes how we think of our self and others. In addition, we know from societal norms when someone is out of step or "weird."

We don't require formal lessons to learn from the messages that bombard us. We take it all in, rather uncritically.

With all these messages about how to behave

floating around, it is extremely hard to know who you are. It is easy to "lose" your self while trying to meet everyone else's expectations.

The solution to this problem is personal insight in the form of experimentation combined with awareness. If you can put your self in a wide variety of situations and stay tuned to (aware of) how you feel in each, you can start to figure out what you genuinely like and what you genuinely dislike.

To figure out what you genuinely like, you must ignore any desire to please others. You must focus in on your own likes and dislikes. Knowing what you genuinely like and dislike is critical to knowing who you are.

In a relationship, your likes and dislikes become a guide for answering the question: am I allowed to be myself, and am I staying true to myself?

It is important to note that what you like and dislike can and will change over time. As it changes, who you are also changes. That is normal.

More on who you are will follow. It is now time to consider going forward.

<u>Part Three</u>
Going Forward

Going Forward

☼

"Do not fear going forward slowly; fear only to stand
still."
Chinese Proverb

Visualizing Your New Partner:

The first step in going forward is to literally
visualize your new partner. As you understand your
own likes and dislikes better, visualize a partner who
has similar likes and dislikes.

Do not imagine someone with exactly the same
likes and dislikes. It is improbable that such a person
exists, we are all too unique.

When it seems like you have met someone who
has exactly the same likes and dislikes, it is more
likely that this person is suppressing his or her true
likes and dislikes to give a false sense of
compatibility. Being in a relationship with this type
of person inevitably leads to trouble as the person's
true likes and dislikes emerge, causing uncertainty
about who exactly your new partner is.

Do imagine someone with similar likes and dislikes, particularly when your own likes and dislikes are a high priority to you.

For example, if staying physically fit is a high priority to you, imagine someone with a similar emphasis on staying fit. In contrast, if having a "status" car is a low priority to you, you should avoid imagining a partner who places a high priority on driving around in a high status car.

As you may have already noted, imagining a future partner takes some effort. You must start from your own likes and dislikes, then think of what a partner with compatible likes and dislikes will be like. You can start with basic characteristics like visualizing someone who you are physically attracted to, who is trustworthy, and who is available. Then move on to add features that are of high priority to you. For example, interest in getting married, interest in having children, interest in balancing career and family, interest in travel, and so on.

Draw a mental picture with as much detail as you can muster. Revisit the picture you have created often. If it helps, write down the likes and dislikes of a future partner as well as any other characteristics you are imagining. The better job you do visualizing a new partner, the more likely you are to find such a person.

Why is this so? If you know about the law of attraction, you might think I am recommending visualizing a new partner so that your energy or "vibrational level" can "attract" such a person to you. If the universe works this way, great!

If the universe does not work as the law of attraction dictates, it is still important to visualize a new partner because it is difficult to "see" what you cannot visualize or imagine. Think of all the times "hindsight" lets you see something after the fact. If you visualize something beforehand, you are much more likely to see it as it is happening.

In addition, visualizing a new partner fights two human tendencies that limit our relationships. The first of these two tendencies is to avoid the complex details of other people's lives. An obvious example of this tendency at work is the phenomena of prejudice-- when how we think and feel about someone else is based on superficial characteristics or group affiliation (religious group, political party, etc.). When we avoid thinking about the complex details of another's life, we cannot "know" them, and we certainly won't be able to "see" them for who they are.

Instead of visualizing a "Christian" (or Jewish or Muslim) partner, think more deeply about what values such a partner would hold dear. Would he or she follow the "Golden Rule"--do unto others as you would have them do unto you? Would he or she believe deeply in "giving back" and in a forgiving "God?" The point is that the more detail you create when visualizing a future partner, the easier it will be to "see" those details or characteristics when they exist in someone new.

If you are willing and able to do this, you will find it easier to recognize a new partner when he or she comes along. You will have fought off the human tendency to simplify and thereby distort the true nature of others. And, you efforts will pay off in choosing to relate to someone based on a more thorough understanding of who they are.

The second human tendency that deserves mention is the tendency to gravitate toward relationships that are familiar, even if what is familiar is abusive and unhealthy relationships.

It is a fact that familiarity produces comfort. We are all more comfortable with what is known and predictable than we are with what is unknown and unpredictable. It is a sad fact that familiarity in relating to others and the comfort familiarity provides can limit us to the kinds of relationships we have already had, even if they have been bad.

Too often a relationship starts and gains momentum with a partner who exhibits behaviors and attitudes that are simultaneously familiar and troubling. For example, a woman will fall in love with a man who has familiar personality traits to her alcoholic father. Whether the man abuses alcohol or not at the time they meet, she is stuck in a dysfunctional but familiar relationship. The familiarity provides comfort, but at the expense of dysfunction.

The solution to the tendency to gravitate toward the familiar when the familiar is unwanted is to visualize a partner who relates in a way that is desirable and functional or healthy. This is not as difficult as it may sound. No doubt, someone has related to you positively during the course of your life, even if only briefly.

Visualize a partner who relates to you positively the majority, if not the vast majority, of the time. Imagine how you will feel if someone is consistently supportive and loving to you. Imagine a loving and healthy relationship as a possibility. Imagine it enough to get familiar with it.

Many will find themselves feeling uncomfortable when imagining such a relationship. They, and perhaps you, will start to wait for the "other shoe to drop." The uncertainty of what will happen can take hold and drive individuals back to the familiar. This is why people have the same kind of dysfunctional relationships over and over. It is why children who come from abusive homes often cling to their abusive parents. In their minds it is better to stay with the familiar and relatively predictable abuser than risk an unfamiliar and unpredictable and potential abuser.

The task is to visualize being comfortable with some uncertainty as well as to imagine a relationship with someone who is consistently supportive and loving.

If you are able to complete this task, you may also find that you do not require the kind of constant reassurance from your partner that tends to drive people away. Constant reassurance is only necessary if you think your partner is likely to emotionally withdraw or to otherwise abandon you.

Visualize a different kind of partner so that you can see him or her when she comes along and you can tolerate any unfamiliarity you have with a relationship with someone who is consistently loving toward you.

I cannot guarantee you will never be hurt by someone who seems at first, and maybe even for a long time, to be consistently loving and supportive.

People change and things happen. On the other hand, I can guarantee that you will not enter into a healthy and positive relationship unless you are able to visualize it first--unless, of course, it happens by accident. Do you really want to leave it up to chance?

In summary, visualizing a future partner and the type of relationship you would like, in detail, helps you "see" this partner when he or she comes into your life. In addition, visualizing a future, consistently positive relationship helps you to better tolerate the uncertainty inherent in all relationships, even relationships that are unfamiliar but wonderful.

Consolidating Who You Are:

Consolidating who you are means continuing to explore your likes and dislikes while adding other dimensions of you to your sense of who you are.

Your likes and dislikes are an important way of summarizing who you are. Arguably, it is the most important way. Nonetheless, a complete picture of who you are also incorporates an accounting of your talents, your limitations, your fears and worries, what motivates you, your unique experiences, and your unique perspective.

Your likes and dislikes are influenced by your

experiences, perspective, talents, limitations, motivation, and your fears and worries. In turn, your likes and dislikes influence your perspective, motivation, and your fears and worries.

Because of their central role, likes and dislikes summarize you better than any description of your talent, motivation, experiences, or fears and worries. But your likes and dislikes are not all there is to you.

So, in addition, to liking people who live by the Golden Rule, you might be a talented musician or good at listening to others.

The point is that you will never just be a summary of your likes and dislikes, even though, when it comes to relationships, the focus should be on who you are as discovered by examining your likes and dislikes. In other words, your likes and dislikes are not all there is to you, but they do have more to do with satisfaction in relating to others than your talents, past experiences, perspective, and your fears and worries.

Please note that, of course, your likes and dislikes are likely to evolve or change over time. The formula for figuring out who you are by taking stock of your likes and dislikes will not change, however.

In summary, create as comprehensive a mental picture or image of who you are as you can. Start with the descriptive stuff like what your talents are, what you fear, how you see the world, and so on. Finish your image with an accounting of your likes and dislikes. The image you create is the "you," you bring to a new love.

<u>Part Four</u>
New Love

New Love

☼

"This bud of love, by summer's ripening breath,
May prove a beauteous flower when next we meet."
William Shakespeare (1564 – 1616)
"Romeo and Juliet"

Being True to Your Self:

By this point you've hopefully learned that forming a successful relationship takes more than just being physically attracted to someone. Physical attraction certainly plays a role, but hopefully along with that, you will know who you are, and you will have a clear notion of what a good partner brings in the way of personal characteristics and relationship priorities.

If you really want to avoid the emotional pain or feelings of despair that follow a breakup, you need to pay attention to being and staying true to your self. This means knowing your likes and dislikes and not suppressing or "spinning" them to convince your self or a partner of how ideal, compatible, "well-suited," or perfect you are as a couple.

It is possible to sustain a "false" self for a while. It is also possible to shift or edit your likes and dislikes. But after the "bloom" is off the rose of "love," you will have to deal with your true likes and dislikes or suffer in silence. Being "untrue" to your self will sooner or later put you into a kind of "hell on earth."

I'm not saying that most relationships are doomed because one or both partners suppress their "true selves." As with anything, there are degrees of how much individuals distort their "true self." I think it is fair to say, however, the greater the degree of distortion, the more troubled the relationship is likely to be over the long term.

Start your new relationship right by being true to your self as much as possible. Take advantage of the work you have done to know your self well. Mild distortions are not likely to cause a breakup in otherwise good relationships, but major distortions will lead to trouble. Would you not rather say, "he/she loves me as I am," than "I only pretended to like football (dogs, hunting, skiing, the opera, etc.) because I wanted you to like me."

When to Start a New Relationship:

In all my years of working with people on relationship "issues," no one waited as long as I or other "experts" recommended before starting a new relationship. In general, the advice was to wait six to eighteen months before starting a new relationship. Six months being offered as a minimum for recovering from a "serious" relationship.

The six to eighteen months would ideally be spent reaching a point of acceptance and getting reacquainted with one's self as a single person. The time would ideally also be devoted to figuring out personal likes and dislikes and visualizing a new partner.

In contrast to the advice, people sometimes started a new relationship literally days after a breakup. The determining factors seemed to be availability of a new partner and not wanting to be alone.

If a new partner was not readily available, the energy went into finding one. Sometimes jumping into a new relationship doomed the individual to another relationship loss; sometimes not.

No matter how many times you need to take to learn this lesson, learn it eventually: while no relationship is without its challenges, your best chance of having a successful relationship is through combining (1) the insight of knowing who you are and what a healthy relationship looks like with (2) the practice of remaining true to your self from the outset.

Spend enough time between relationships to figure out what your true likes and dislikes are, not what others tell you they should be. Spend enough time to be familiar with your visualized version of a new love or partner. Finally, spend enough time to gain the confidence to say, "This is who I am. Love me as I am or there's the door."

If you want to have a life of serial relationships, that is your business. Don't expect to escape the emotional pain of a lost love, however. If you want to explore deeper, committed love, then spend the months and years it might take to know who you are and what a healthy relationship looks like.

Relationship Success:

Relationship success can be as simple as relating to someone else without distorting who you are, while maintaining genuine and mutual caring and support. The relationship may last minutes or a lifetime. It may be exclusive or not.

For most of us, a successful relationship also has other features, including exclusivity and longevity. These types of successful relationships are something two people have to work at. In addition, successful, healthy relationships usually require that the partners remain committed to being "in relationship" as much as they remain committed to each other.

This means that at some point each partner decides that preserving the relationship is important even though he or she has considered breaking up with the other partner.

I think what people come to realize is that a relationship is more than the sum of its parts and that they have a role in any relationship difficulties. These realizations cause partners to commit to being "in relationship" and to working on their relationship skills. This is instead of leaving a partner in the hope that a new partner and new relationship will work better despite the "baggage" they bring to it.

Of course, things do not always work this way, and lots of relationships end. At the same time, few people who have serial relationships escape reliving the same kind of issues that they had in a past relationship(s). Their "relationship baggage" inevitably emerges because they have not examined their role in creating any difficulties.

You can reduce the work involved in being in a long-term relationship by observing the following advice from the start: know your self, know what a healthy relationship looks like, and be true to your self. Work will inevitably need to be done, however, as feelings, likes, and dislikes change.

With this background in mind, please note that successful relationships have many characteristics in common. The more important of these characteristics are:

- Both partners are respectful and supportive of each other's likes and dislikes. Their high priority or core likes and dislikes are compatible, and any differences are viewed as unique and special characteristics that make the partner interesting.

- Personal agendas are negotiated with an eye toward compromise and preserving the interests of each partner. If one partner needs to do something that is in conflict with the other, the differences are worked out amicably and with respect for each other's needs.

- Neither partner has narcissistic personal needs that create an imbalance in how much importance the other partner's needs are given. For example, one partner's need to flirt does not outweigh the other partner's need to feel secure in the relationship.

- The partners have been able to evolve from their past relationship experiences or "imprints" and form new and healthier imprints. For example, the man whose mother was consistently critical of him has evolved in his thinking about relationships and no longer falls for hypercritical women because that is what his imprint is.

- Finally, the partners are able to evolve as individuals at a rate that maintains their compatibility.

Successful relationships start with falling in love but sustain themselves with mutual respect, caring, and support. It's been said[8] that there are only two reasons to have a long-term relationship. The first is because two people in a caring relationship have more resources to work with, when raising children, than a single adult. The second is because of the "friction." The point is that successful relationships spur us to be better people through conflict (friction). This is as long as the conflict occurs in a place of ultimate safety established by mutual respect, caring,

---

8 M. Scott Peck author of *The Road Less Traveled*.

and support.

You can have a successful relationship! Increase your chances by knowing your genuine likes and dislikes, staying true to your self, and having a clear image of a future partner and a healthy relationship with this partner.

Part Five

In Summary

In Summary

☼

"A good book has no ending."
R. D. Cumming (1917-2004)

In Summary:

Ideal or optimal relationships do not happen without some insight into what makes one's self and others "tick." They do not happen between people who are not true to themselves. They do not happen between relationship "naturals," if such people exist outside the fantasy of movies and television. Ideal or optimal relationships do happen between people who know themselves and work at knowing and caring for others.

This book has focused on both recovering from the loss of a relationship and on forming a new, more satisfying future relationship. The underlying orientation has been on what you can do to make your self healthier and better at initiating and sustaining a more ideal relationship. The hope has been to increase your personal insight into how and why you relate in the way you do.

Five steps were described. The steps are: (1) taking care of one's physical and emotional self, (2) accepting the loss of a relationship; a lost love, (3) getting to know "who you are," (4) spending time visualizing a future partner and a relationship with him or her, and (5) staying true to your self from the outset of a new relationship.

In many ways, this book is just a starting point to recovering from a relationship loss and working toward a new love relationship. It is akin to the foundation and framework of a new house. There is some finishing work to be done that is specific to your individual situation, needs, and desires.

Email consultation and the Self Help In Sight blog are available for you to start building on the start the book offers. You may also take a "relationship readiness" survey at selfhelpinsight.com. Please read the blog and contact me to assist with your relationship self-help effort .

Index

About the Author

Dr. Lebo is a licensed psychologist who has been practicing for twenty years. From his earliest days in graduate school, he was interested in helping people who do just fine, do better. Not content with focusing on only healing "illness," he supplemented his coursework and training with articles and books on highly functional individuals and their strategies for doing better than average. This research revealed ideas about "self" and "self in relationship" with others that promote healthy self-image and relationships. These ideas have been refined over the course of twenty years of working with individuals in a clinical setting.

You may reach Dr. Lebo by email at <u>drlebo@selfhelpinsight.com</u>.